THIS BOOK BELONGS TO

_____

START DATE

_____

SHE READS TRUTH

EXECUTIVE

FOUNDER/CHIEF EXECUTIVE OFFICER
Raechel Myers

CO-FOUNDER/CHIEF CONTENT OFFICER
Amanda Bible Williams

CHIEF OPERATING OFFICER
Ryan Myers

EXECUTIVE ASSISTANT
Sarah Andereck

EDITORIAL

EDITORIAL DIRECTOR
Jessica Lamb

CONTENT EDITOR
Kara Gause

ASSOCIATE EDITORS
Bailey Gillespie
Tameshia Williams

EDITORIAL ASSISTANT
Hannah Little

CREATIVE

CREATIVE DIRECTOR
Jeremy Mitchell

LEAD DESIGNER
Kelsea Allen

DESIGNERS
Abbey Benson
Davis DeLisi
Annie Glover

MARKETING

MARKETING DIRECTOR
Krista Juline Williams

MARKETING MANAGER
Katie Matuska Pierce

COMMUNITY SUPPORT SPECIALIST
Margot Williams

SHIPPING & LOGISTICS

LOGISTICS MANAGER
Lauren Gloyne

SHIPPING MANAGER
Sydney Bess

CUSTOMER SUPPORT SPECIALIST
Katy McKnight

FULFILLMENT SPECIALISTS
Abigail Achord
Cait Baggerman

SUBSCRIPTION INQUIRIES
orders@shereadstruth.com

CONTRIBUTORS

COVER PHOTOGRAPHY
Janessa Spina Higgins

PHOTOGRAPHY
Janessa Spina Higgins (52)
Lindsey Stewart (78)
Raisa Zwart (28, 44, 68)

@SHEREADSTRUTH

Download the
She Reads Truth app,
available for iOS
and Android

Subscribe to the
She Reads Truth podcast

SHEREADSTRUTH.COM

SHE READS TRUTH™

© 2021 by She Reads Truth, LLC

All rights reserved.

All photography used by permission.

ISBN 978-1-952670-16-9

1 2 3 4 5 6 7 8 9 10

All Scripture is taken from the Christian Standard Bible®. Copyright © 2020 by Holman Bible Publishers. Used by permission. Christian Standard Bible® and CSB® are federally registered trademarks of Holman Bible Publishers.

Research support provided by Logos Bible Software™. Learn more at logos.com.

Though the dates and locations in this book have been carefully researched, scholars disagree on the dating and locations of many biblical events.

This book was printed offset in Nashville, Tennessee, on 70# Lynx Opaque. Cover is 100# Cougar Opaque with a soft touch lamination.

1 & 2 THESSALONIANS

SHE READS TRUTH

WE NEED ONE ANOTHER AS A
TESTIMONY OF WHAT CHRIST HAS
ALREADY ACCOMPLISHED AND AS
A REMINDER THAT HIS WORK IN US
AND IN CREATION IS NOT DONE.

Jessica

Jessica Lamb
EDITORIAL DIRECTOR

Word debates have a tendency to bring out strong feelings from our editorial team. Though our section of the office (a.k.a. "Editorial Alley") is known for being good-natured, we are quick to draw our proofing pens and stet stamps for a stand-off only Merriam-Webster can settle.

More troublesome are those words still waiting on a ruling from our dictionaries: is the word for "improving by making slight adjustments" spelled *zhuzh, tszuj,* or *zhoosh*? Sometimes, the preference is regional. As a native Arkansasan who grew up in Texas, my affection for the word *y'all* used to make our Pennsylvanian content editor raise both an eyebrow and a red pen. After years in the South, though, she's come around, declaring that *y'all* has permeated our culture, pitched a tent in our hearts, and started handing out free sweet tea to all passersby.

First & 2 Thessalonians are part of why I hold such affection for *y'all* and all its collective goodness. These letters are brimming with statements addressing "you"—but not a single one refers to an individual. Every time, Paul is addressing the collective *y'all*, so to speak. When we read in 1 Thessalonians 5:16–18 to "rejoice always, pray constantly, give thanks in everything; for this is God's will for you in Christ Jesus," we are reading about God's desire for His people, the Church, to pursue these things together. As you read, use the study prompts on page 15 to see how each of these three commands are woven throughout these letters, your life, and your faith community.

For a weary Paul and Silvanus, in the midst of distress and affliction on a missionary journey in Macedonia (see a map of this journey on page 22), Timothy's report on the Thessalonians' continued faith was a source of unexpected joy and life. Paul wrote to them with compassionate correction and reminders of Jesus's return, encouraging them to persevere through persecution and doctrinal misunderstandings.

Christ has made us a family—brothers and sisters through His blood and the work of the Holy Spirit. Christian community is a gift to us, and we are each meant to be a gift to the Church as well. We need one another as a testimony of what Christ has already accomplished and as a reminder that His work in us and in creation is not done.

Whether you prefer *y'all, you lot, youse, you guys, you-uns,* or something else altogether, read these epistles remembering that, in Christ, you are more than just an "I" or a singular "you." You are part of a global, local, and historic "we." The greatest gift we can offer one another is our united hope in Christ. We are His. And as we wait together for His return, He is still at work in us, around us, and through us.

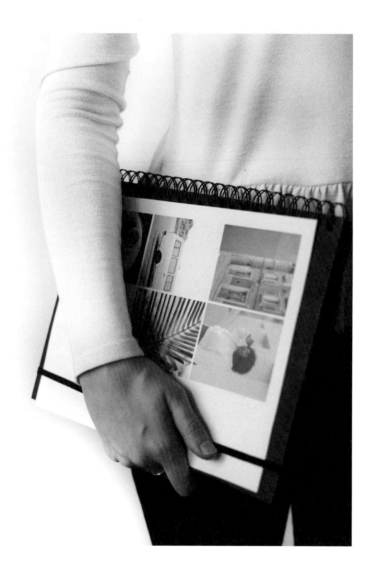

At She Reads Truth, we believe in pairing the inherently beautiful Word of God with the aesthetic beauty it deserves. Each of our resources is thoughtfully and artfully designed to highlight the beauty, goodness, and truth of Scripture in a way that reflects the themes of each curated reading plan.

For our 1 & 2 Thessalonians reading plan, we used high-contrast photography to express the hope we can have even while enduring difficult seasons. Visual moments of stillness remind us that even when we don't see change happening, God is still working as we persevere in our faith.

A warm color palette reflects Paul's love for the Thessalonian believers, which he expresses throughout these two letters. With the joyful movement of its swashes and ligatures, the Rosie font calls back to Paul's encouragement to keep going.

ROSIE

ABCDEFG
HIJKLMNO
PQRSTUV
WXY&Z

LIGHT

PANTONE®

HOW TO USE THIS BOOK

She Reads Truth is a community of women dedicated to reading the Word of God every day. The Bible is living and active, and we confidently hold it higher than anything we can do or say.

READ & REFLECT

This **1 & 2 Thessalonians** Study Book focuses primarily on Scripture, with bonus resources to facilitate deeper engagement with God's Word.

SCRIPTURE READING

Designed for a Monday start, this Study Book presents the books of 1 & 2 Thessalonians in daily readings, with supplemental passages for additional context.

REFLECTION QUESTIONS

Each week features questions for personal reflection.

COMMUNITY & CONVERSATION

Join women from Zionsville, IN, to Zimbabwe as they read with you!

 SHE READS TRUTH APP

Devotionals corresponding to each daily reading can be found in the **1 & 2 Thessalonians** reading plan on the She Reads Truth app. You can also participate in community discussions, download free lock screens for Weekly Truth memorization, and more.

GRACE DAY

Use Saturdays to catch up on your reading, pray, and rest in the presence of the Lord.

WEEKLY TRUTH

Sundays are set aside for Scripture memorization.

EXTRAS

This book features additional tools to help you gain a deeper understanding of the text.

See a complete list of extras on page 13.

SHEREADSTRUTH.COM

All of our reading plans and devotionals are also available at SheReadsTruth.com. Invite your family, friends, and neighbors to read along with you!

SHE READS TRUTH PODCAST

Join our She Reads Truth founders and their guests each Monday as they open their Bibles and talk about the beauty, goodness, and truth they find there. Subscribe to the podcast so you don't miss conversations about the current community reading plan.

TABLE ^{OF} CONTENTS

WEEK TWO

2

WEEK THREE

3

EXTRAS

REJOICE ALWAYS, PRAY CONSTANTLY, GIVE THANKS IN EVERYTHING; FOR THIS IS GOD'S WILL FOR YOU IN CHRIST JESUS.

1 THESSALONIANS 5:16–18

STUDY PROMPTS

In 1 Thessalonians 5:16–18, the apostle Paul called the church at Thessalonica to live out God's will for their lives by faithfully implementing three practices. As you read 1 & 2 Thessalonians over the next three weeks, pay careful attention to Paul's commands to rejoice, pray, and give thanks by using the following study prompts. (You may not end up using these marks every day!)

Rejoice
pray
give thanks

1

Place an exclamation point in the margin next to any commands to rejoice or examples of rejoicing.

2

Draw a square around any commands to pray or examples of prayer.

3

Draw a circle around any commands to give thanks or examples of thanksgiving.

1 THESSALONIANS

Rejoice always, pray constantly, give thanks in everything; for this is God's will for you in Christ Jesus.

1 THESSALONIANS 5:16–18

First Thessalonians can be reliably dated to AD 50 or 51, between Paul's second and third missionary journeys.

A LITTLE BACKGROUND

Thessalonica was the capital city and a major port of the Roman province of Macedonia, with a population of about 200,000. Loyal to Caesar, Thessalonica was filled with pagan worshipers of idols, the full pantheon of Greek and Roman gods, and was well known for its emperor worship.

MESSAGE & PURPOSE

Timothy reported to Paul that although the church at Thessalonica was suffering affliction, they were holding fast to the faith. Though they had some doctrinal misunderstandings, they were laboring for the Lord out of love and patiently hoping for the return of Christ. Paul wrote to encourage the church in their faith, to remind them that sanctification was God's will for them, and to correct misunderstandings about end-time events.

First Thessalonians presents four major themes:

1 THE CONDUCT OF PAUL'S MINISTRY

Paul's ministry centered on two aspects: the communication of the Word of God and the sharing of his life (1Th 2:8). Paul's motives were to please God (1Th 2:4; 4:1) and to express his concern for the Thessalonians' welfare (1Th 2:8).

2 PERSECUTION

The Thessalonian church was founded in the midst of persecution. Paul encouraged the believers there to stand firm and not be shaken by these afflictions because Christians are "going to experience affliction" (1Th 3:3–4).

3 SANCTIFICATION

The process of sanctification begins once a person believes in Christ and receives forgiveness of sins. Paul's prayer for the believers at Thessalonica was that God would make their hearts "blameless in holiness" before God (1Th 3:13).

4 THE SECOND COMING OF CHRIST

Jesus's return is mentioned in every chapter of 1 Thessalonians.

GIVE THANKS FOR
THE BOOK OF 1
THESSALONIANS

First Thessalonians contributes to our understanding of the second coming of Christ. Paul wrote to correct misunderstandings of this doctrine, and in the process showed us that Christ's return gives us true hope.

PAUL'S MINISTRY TO THESSALONICA

You'll notice the Scripture reading for today is longer than the others. These chapters from the book of Acts provide context for our study of 1 & 2 Thessalonians.

Timothy
- Jew/greek
- highly regarded

ACTS 16
PAUL SELECTS TIMOTHY

[1] Paul went on to Derbe and Lystra, where there was a disciple named Timothy, the son of a believing Jewish woman, but his father was a Greek. [2] The brothers and sisters at Lystra and Iconium spoke highly of him. [3] Paul wanted Timothy to go with him; so he took him and circumcised him because of the Jews who were in those places, since they all knew that his father was a Greek. [4] As they traveled through the towns, they delivered the decisions reached by the apostles and elders at Jerusalem for the people to observe. [5] So the churches were strengthened in the faith and grew daily in numbers.

EVANGELIZATION OF EUROPE

[6] They went through the region of Phrygia and Galatia; they had been forbidden by the Holy Spirit to speak the word in Asia. [7] When they came to Mysia, they tried to go into Bithynia, but the Spirit of Jesus did not allow them. [8] Passing by Mysia they went down to Troas. [9] During the night Paul had a vision in which a Macedonian man was standing and pleading with him, "Cross over to Macedonia and help us!" [10] After he had seen the vision, we immediately made efforts to set out for Macedonia, concluding that God had called us to preach the gospel to them.

LYDIA'S CONVERSION

[11] From Troas we put out to sea and sailed straight for Samothrace, the next day to Neapolis, [12] and from there to Philippi, a Roman colony and a leading city of the district of Macedonia. We stayed in that city for several days. [13] On the Sabbath day we went outside the city gate by the river, where we expected to find a place of prayer. We sat down and spoke to the women gathered there. [14] A God-fearing woman named Lydia, a dealer in purple cloth from the city of Thyatira, was listening. The Lord opened her heart to respond to what Paul was saying. [15] After she and her household were baptized, she urged us, "If you consider me a believer in the Lord, come and stay at my house." And she persuaded us.

PAUL AND SILAS IN PRISON

[16] Once, as we were on our way to prayer, a slave girl met us who had a spirit by which she predicted the future. She made a large profit for her owners by fortune-telling. [17] As she followed Paul and us she cried out, "These men, who are proclaiming to you a way of salvation, are the servants of the Most High God." [18] She did this for many days.

Paul was greatly annoyed. Turning to the spirit, he said, "I command you in the name of Jesus Christ to come out of her!" And it came out right away.

[19] When her owners realized that their hope of profit was gone, they seized Paul and Silas and dragged them into the marketplace to the authorities. [20] Bringing them before the chief magistrates, they said, "These men are seriously disturbing our city. They are Jews [21] and are promoting customs that are not legal for us as Romans to adopt or practice." [22] The crowd joined in the attack against them, and the chief magistrates stripped off their clothes and ordered them to be beaten with rods. [23] After they had severely flogged them, they threw them in jail, ordering the jailer to guard them carefully. [24] Receiving such an order, he put them into the inner prison and secured their feet in the stocks.

A MIDNIGHT DELIVERANCE *amidst imprisonment*

[25] About midnight Paul and Silas were praying and singing hymns to God, and the prisoners were listening to them. [26] Suddenly there was such a violent earthquake that the foundations of the jail were shaken, and immediately all the doors were opened, and everyone's chains came loose. [27] When the jailer woke up and saw the doors of the prison standing open, he drew his sword and was going to kill himself, since he thought the prisoners had escaped.

[28] But Paul called out in a loud voice, "Don't harm yourself, because we're all here!"

[29] The jailer called for lights, rushed in, and fell down trembling before Paul and Silas. [30] He escorted them out and said, "Sirs, what must I do to be saved?"

[31] They said, "Believe in the Lord Jesus, and you will be saved—you and your household." [32] And they spoke the word of the Lord to him along with everyone in his house.

in the freedom in the midst of a hard moment. God was glorified

³³ He took them the same hour of the night and washed their wounds. Right away he and all his family were baptized. ³⁴ He brought them into his house, set a meal before them, and rejoiced because he had come to believe in God with his entire household.

AN OFFICIAL APOLOGY

³⁵ When daylight came, the chief magistrates sent the police to say, "Release those men."

³⁶ The jailer reported these words to Paul: "The magistrates have sent orders for you to be released. So come out now and go in peace."

³⁷ But Paul said to them, "They beat us in public without a trial, although we are Roman citizens, and threw us in jail. And now are they going to send us away secretly? Certainly not! On the contrary, let them come themselves and escort us out."

³⁸ The police reported these words to the magistrates. They were afraid when they heard that Paul and Silas were Roman citizens. ³⁹ So they came to appease them, and escorting them from prison, they urged them to leave town. ⁴⁰ After leaving the jail, they came to Lydia's house, where they saw and encouraged the brothers and sisters, and departed.

ACTS 17:1-9
A SHORT MINISTRY IN THESSALONICA

¹ After they passed through Amphipolis and Apollonia, they came to Thessalonica, where there was a Jewish synagogue. ² As usual, Paul went into the synagogue, and on three Sabbath days reasoned with them from the Scriptures, ³ explaining and proving that it was necessary for the Messiah to suffer and rise from the dead: "This Jesus I am proclaiming to you is the Messiah." ⁴ Some of them were persuaded and joined Paul and Silas, including a large number of God-fearing Greeks, as well as a number of the leading women.

RIOT IN THE CITY

⁵ But the Jews became jealous, and they brought together some wicked men from the marketplace, formed a mob, and started a riot in the city. Attacking Jason's house, they searched for them to bring them out to the public assembly. ⁶ When they did not find them, they dragged Jason and some of the brothers before the city officials, shouting, "These men who have turned the world upside down have come here too, ⁷ and Jason has welcomed them. They are all acting contrary to Caesar's decrees, saying that there is another king—Jesus." ⁸ The crowd and city officials who heard these things were upset. ⁹ After taking a security bond from Jason and the others, they released them.

THIS JESUS I AM PROCLAIMING TO YOU IS THE MESSIAH.

ACTS 17:3

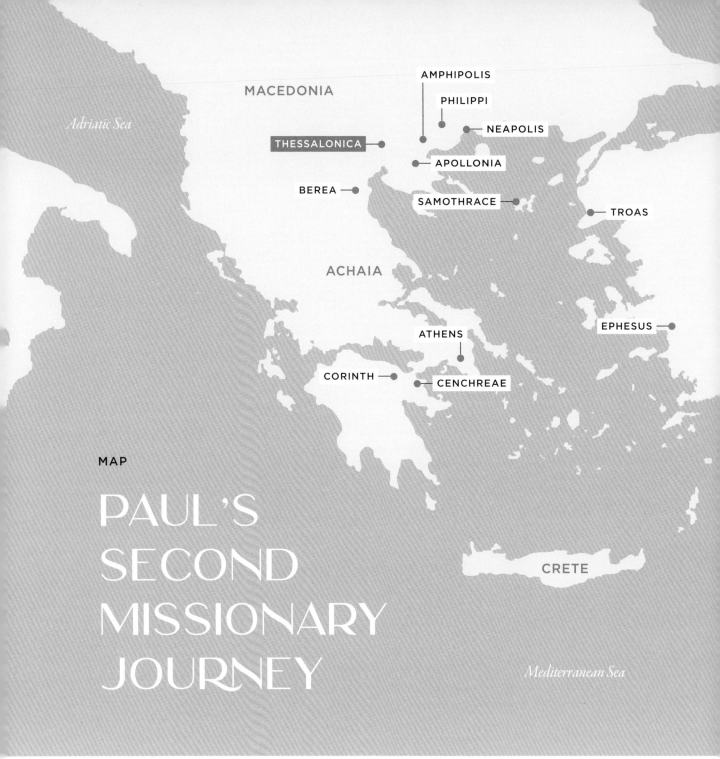

MACEDONIA

Adriatic Sea

AMPHIPOLIS

PHILIPPI

NEAPOLIS

THESSALONICA

APOLLONIA

BEREA

SAMOTHRACE

TROAS

ACHAIA

ATHENS

EPHESUS

CORINTH

CENCHREAE

MAP

PAUL'S SECOND MISSIONARY JOURNEY

CRETE

Mediterranean Sea

The apostle Paul's second missionary journey took him, along with Timothy and Silas, deep into the heart of the Roman Empire as they brought the gospel to major cities like Athens and Corinth. During this trip, Paul founded the church in Thessalonica, to whom 1 & 2 Thessalonians were written.

ANTIOCH   LYSTRA   SAMOTHRACE

DERBE   TROAS

GALATIA

CAPPADOCIA

ASIA
MINOR

LYSTRA

DERBE

PAMPHYLIA

ANTIOCH

CYPRUS

CAESAREA

SAMARIA

JERUSALEM

JUDEA

N

0 MI   100   200
0 KM   100   200   300

PHILIPPI   APOLLONIA   BEREA   CORINTH   EPHESUS   JERUSALEM

NEAPOLIS   AMPHIPOLIS   THESSALONICA   ATHENS   CENCHREAE   CAESAREA   ANTIOCH

rejoice
pray
give thanks

FAITH AMID PERSECUTION

1 THESSALONIANS

1 THESSALONIANS 1
GREETING

[1] Paul, Silvanus, and Timothy:

To the church of the Thessalonians in God the Father and the Lord Jesus Christ.

Grace to you and peace.

thanks

THANKSGIVING

[2] We always thank God for all of you, making mention of you constantly in our prayers. [3] We recall, in the presence of our God and Father, your work produced by faith, your labor motivated by love, and your endurance inspired by hope in our Lord Jesus Christ. [4] For we know, brothers and sisters loved by God, that he has chosen you, [5] because our gospel did not come to you in word only, but also in power, in the Holy Spirit, and with full assurance. You know how we lived among you for your benefit, [6] and you yourselves became imitators of us and of the Lord when, in spite of severe persecution, you welcomed the message with joy from the

prayers

faith
love
hope

Holy Spirit. [7] As a result, you became an example to all the believers in Macedonia and Achaia. [8] For the word of the Lord rang out from you, not only in Macedonia and Achaia, but in every place that your faith in God has gone out. Therefore, we don't need to say anything, [9] for they themselves report what kind of reception we had from you: how you turned to God from idols to serve the living and true God [10] and to wait for his Son from heaven, whom he raised from the dead—Jesus, who rescues us from the coming wrath.

ROMANS 8:35-39

[35] Who can separate us from the love of Christ? Can affliction or distress or persecution or famine or nakedness or danger or sword? [36] As it is written:

Because of you
we are being put to death all day long;
we are counted as sheep to be slaughtered.

[37] No, in all these things we are more than conquerors through him who loved us. [38] For I am persuaded that neither death nor life, nor angels nor rulers, nor things present nor things to come, nor powers, [39] nor height nor depth, nor any other created thing will be able to separate us from the love of God that is in Christ Jesus our Lord.

1 PETER 4:12-14
CHRISTIAN SUFFERING

[12] Dear friends, don't be surprised when the fiery ordeal comes among you to test you, as if something unusual were happening to you. [13] Instead, rejoice as you share in the sufferings of Christ, so that you may also rejoice with great joy when his glory is revealed. [14] If you are ridiculed for the name of Christ, you are blessed, because the Spirit of glory and of God rests on you.

NOTES

v7 → domino effect of faith, love & hope.
v9 → turned from idols to God
v10 → awaiting Jesus' return

WALKING
WORTHY
OF GOD

1 THESSALONIANS

1 THESSALONIANS 2:1–12
PAUL'S CONDUCT

[1] For you yourselves know, brothers and sisters, that our visit with you was not without result. [2] On the contrary, after we had previously suffered and were treated outrageously in Philippi, as you know, we were emboldened by our God to speak the gospel of God to you in spite of great opposition. [3] For our exhortation didn't come from error or impurity or an intent to deceive. [4] Instead, just as we have been approved by God to be entrusted with the gospel, so we speak, not to please people, but rather God, who examines our hearts. [5] For we never used flattering speech, as you know, or had greedy motives—God is our witness— [6] and we didn't seek glory from people, either from you or from others. [7] Although we could have been a burden as Christ's apostles, instead we were gentle among you, as a nurse nurtures her own children. [8] We cared so much for you that we were pleased to share with you not only the gospel of God but also our own lives, because you had become dear to us. [9] For you remember our labor and hardship, brothers and sisters. Working night and day so that we would not burden any of you, we preached God's gospel to you. [10] You are witnesses, and so is God, of how devoutly, righteously, and blamelessly we conducted ourselves with you believers. [11] As you know, like a father with his own children, [12] we encouraged, comforted, and implored each one of you to walk worthy of God, who calls you into his own kingdom and glory.

LUKE 6:43–45
A TREE AND ITS FRUIT

[43] "A good tree doesn't produce bad fruit; on the other hand, a bad tree doesn't produce good fruit. [44] For each tree is known by its own fruit. Figs aren't gathered from thornbushes, or grapes picked from a bramble bush. [45] A good person produces good out of the good stored up in his heart. An evil person produces evil out of the evil stored up in his heart, for his mouth speaks from the overflow of the heart."

HEBREWS 4:12

For the word of God is living and effective and sharper than any double-edged sword, penetrating as far as the separation of soul and spirit, joints and marrow. It is able to judge the thoughts and intentions of the heart.

NOTES

DAY 4

WELCOMING
THE WORD

1 THESSALONIANS

1 THESSALONIANS 2:13-16
RECEPTION AND OPPOSITION TO THE MESSAGE

[13] This is why we constantly thank God, because when you received the word of God that you heard from us, you welcomed it not as a human message, but as it truly is, the word of God, which also works effectively in you who believe. [14] For you, brothers and sisters, became imitators of God's churches in Christ Jesus that are in Judea, since you have also suffered the same things from people of your own country, just as they did from the Jews [15] who killed the Lord Jesus and the prophets and persecuted us. They displease God and are hostile to everyone, [16] by keeping us from speaking to the Gentiles so that they may be saved. As a result, they are constantly filling up their sins to the limit, and wrath has overtaken them at last.

MATTHEW 13:1-9
THE PARABLE OF THE SOWER

[1] On that day Jesus went out of the house and was sitting by the sea. [2] Such large crowds gathered around him that he got into a boat and sat down, while the whole crowd stood on the shore.

³ Then he told them many things in parables, saying, "Consider the sower who went out to sow. ⁴ As he sowed, some seed fell along the path, and the birds came and devoured them. ⁵ Other seed fell on rocky ground where it didn't have much soil, and it grew up quickly since the soil wasn't deep. ⁶ But when the sun came up, it was scorched, and since it had no root, it withered away. ⁷ Other seed fell among thorns, and the thorns came up and choked it. ⁸ Still other seed fell on good ground and produced fruit: some a hundred, some sixty, and some thirty times what was sown. ⁹ Let anyone who has ears listen."

ACTS 13:44–52

⁴⁴ The following Sabbath almost the whole town assembled to hear the word of the Lord. ⁴⁵ But when the Jews saw the crowds, they were filled with jealousy and began to contradict what Paul was saying, insulting him.

⁴⁶ Paul and Barnabas boldly replied, "It was necessary that the word of God be spoken to you first. Since you reject it and judge yourselves unworthy of eternal life, we are turning to the Gentiles. ⁴⁷ For this is what the Lord has commanded us:

I have made you
a light for the Gentiles
to bring salvation
to the ends of the earth."

⁴⁸ When the Gentiles heard this, they rejoiced and honored the word of the Lord, and all who had been appointed to eternal life believed. ⁴⁹ The word of the Lord spread through the whole region. ⁵⁰ But the Jews incited the prominent God-fearing women and the leading men of the city. They stirred up persecution against Paul and Barnabas and expelled them from their district. ⁵¹ But Paul and Barnabas shook the dust off their feet against them and went to Iconium. ⁵² And the disciples were filled with joy and the Holy Spirit.

WHEN YOU RECEIVED THE WORD OF GOD THAT YOU HEARD FROM US, YOU WELCOMED IT.

1 THESSALONIANS 2:13

THE PAULINE EPISTLES

With thirteen epistles in the New Testament canon, Paul contributed more books to the Bible than any other writer in both the Old and New Testaments. Below are a few details about these letters that Paul penned from AD 48–68.

LETTER FORMAT

1

INTRODUCTION

Identification of senders and recipients

Greeting that includes some variation of the words "grace" and "peace"

Blessing, prayer, or thanksgiving

2

MAIN BODY

Statement of purpose for letter

Teaching, rebuke, correction, encouragement, and/or training

3

CLOSING GREETING

Greeting to individual saints or groups

Benediction

LIKELY LOCATIONS WHERE PAUL WROTE LETTERS

ROME

Ephesians ca AD 61
Philippians ca AD 61
Colossians ca AD 61
Philemon ca AD 61
2 Timothy ca AD 67 or ca AD 68

NICOPOLIS

CORINTH

1 & 2 Thessalonians ca AD 50
Romans AD 57

Titus ca AD 62
1 Timothy ca AD 63

EPHESUS

1 & 2 Corinthians AD 56

ANTIOCH

Galatians ca AD 52

LETTER WORD COUNTS
(in original language)

Average letter length
in the first century
90–200 WORDS

Average length
of Paul's letters
1,300 WORDS

Shortest letter
PHILEMON
335 words

Longest letter
ROMANS
7,114 words

LETTER HIGHLIGHTS

Two categories of recipients

TIMOTHY TITUS PHILEMON
THESSALONIANS
COLOSSIANS PHILIPPIANS EPHESIANS GALATIANS CORINTHIANS ROMANS

INDIVIDUALS

CHURCHES

*Three co-greeters listed
in Paul's introductions*

SOSTHENES

1Co 1:1–3

TIMOTHY

2Co 1:1–2; Php 1:1–2; Col 1:1–2;
1Th 1:1; 2Th 1:1–2; Phm 1–3

SILVANUS

1Th 1:1; 2Th 1:1–2

Five letters written from Roman jail

| EPHESIANS | PHILIPPIANS | COLOSSIANS | PHILEMON | 2 TIMOTHY |

Written during Paul's first imprisonment in Rome,
widely referred to as the prison epistles

Written during Paul's
second imprisonment
in Rome

STRENGTH & ENCOURAGEMENT

1 THESSALONIANS

1 THESSALONIANS 2:17-20
PAUL'S DESIRE TO SEE THEM

[17] But as for us, brothers and sisters, after we were forced to leave you for a short time (in person, not in heart), we greatly desired and made every effort to return and see you face to face. [18] So we wanted to come to you—even I, Paul, time and again—but Satan hindered us. [19] For who is our hope or joy or crown of boasting in the presence of our Lord Jesus at his coming? Is it not you? [20] Indeed you are our glory and joy!

1 THESSALONIANS 3:1-5
ANXIETY IN ATHENS

[1] Therefore, when we could no longer stand it, we thought it was better to be left alone in Athens. [2] And we sent Timothy, our brother and God's coworker in the gospel of Christ, to strengthen and encourage you concerning your faith, [3] so that no one will be shaken by these afflictions. For you yourselves know that we are appointed to this. [4] In fact, when we were with you, we told you in advance that we were going to experience affliction, and as you know, it happened. [5] For this reason, when I could no longer stand it, I also sent him to find out about your faith, fearing that the tempter had tempted you and that our labor might be for nothing.

LAMENTATIONS 3:19-24

[19] Remember my affliction and my homelessness,
the wormwood and the poison.
[20] I continually remember them
and have become depressed.
[21] Yet I call this to mind,
and therefore I have hope:

[22] Because of the LORD's faithful love
we do not perish,
for his mercies never end.
[23] They are new every morning;
great is your faithfulness!
[24] I say, "The LORD is my portion,
therefore I will put my hope in him."

JOHN 14:18-26
THE FATHER, THE SON, AND THE HOLY SPIRIT

[18] "I will not leave you as orphans; I am coming to you. [19] In a little while the world will no longer see me, but you will see me. Because I live, you will live too. [20] On that day you will know that I am in my Father, you are in me, and I am in you.

NOTES

INDEED YOU ARE OUR GLORY AND JOY!

1 THESSALONIANS 2:20

²¹ The one who has my commands and keeps them is the one who loves me. And the one who loves me will be loved by my Father. I also will love him and will reveal myself to him."

²² Judas (not Iscariot) said to him, "Lord, how is it you're going to reveal yourself to us and not to the world?"

²³ Jesus answered, "If anyone loves me, he will keep my word. My Father will love him, and we will come to him and make our home with him. ²⁴ The one who doesn't love me will not keep my words. The word that you hear is not mine but is from the Father who sent me.

²⁵ "I have spoken these things to you while I remain with you. ²⁶ But the Counselor, the Holy Spirit, whom the Father will send in my name, will teach you all things and remind you of everything I have told you."

2 CORINTHIANS 1:3-7
THE GOD OF COMFORT

³ Blessed be the God and Father of our Lord Jesus Christ, the Father of mercies and the God of all comfort. ⁴ He comforts us in all our affliction, so that we may be able to comfort those who are in any kind of affliction, through the comfort we ourselves receive from God. ⁵ For just as the sufferings of Christ overflow to us, so also through Christ our comfort overflows. ⁶ If we are afflicted, it is for your comfort and salvation. If we are comforted, it is for your comfort, which produces in you patient endurance of the same sufferings that we suffer. ⁷ And our hope for you is firm, because we know that as you share in the sufferings, so you will also share in the comfort.

IF WE THINK OF PRAYER AS
THE BREATH IN OUR LUNGS
AND THE BLOOD FROM OUR
HEARTS, WE THINK RIGHTLY.

OSWALD CHAMBERS

REJOICE ALWAYS

Reflect on one or two reasons why following Jesus leads us to rejoice.

PRAY CONSTANTLY

What would it look like to practice constant prayer in the week ahead? Where could you grow in incorporating prayer into your daily rhythm and routine?

GIVE THANKS IN EVERYTHING

What is one thing you learned about God in your 1 Thessalonians reading this week that compels you to give thanks?

DATE

GRACE DAY

DAY 6   WEEK 1

Take this day to catch up on your reading, pray, and rest in the presence of the Lord.

ROMANS 8:38-39

For I am persuaded that neither death nor life, nor angels nor rulers, nor things present nor things to come, nor powers, nor height nor depth, nor any other created thing will be able to separate us from the love of God that is in Christ Jesus our Lord.

WEEKLY TRUTH

DAY 7

Scripture is God-breathed and true. When we memorize it, carry the good news of Jesus with us wherever we go.

Over the course of this reading plan, we will commit a passage from 1 Thessalonians 5 to memory, where Paul calls his readers to action. This week, focus on memorizing the first two verses and the beginning of verse 18. Write the words in the space provided as a reminder to rejoice, pray, and give thanks throughout the day.

1 THESSALONIANS 5:16–18

Rejoice always, pray constantly, give thanks in everything; for this is God's will for you in Christ Jesus.

PRAYER FOR THE CHURCH

1 THESSALONIANS

1 THESSALONIANS 3:6–13
ENCOURAGED BY TIMOTHY

⁶ But now Timothy has come to us from you and brought us good news about your faith and love. He reported that you always have good memories of us and that you long to see us, as we also long to see you. ⁷ Therefore, brothers and sisters, in all our distress and affliction, we were encouraged about you through your faith. ⁸ For now we live, if you stand firm in the Lord. ⁹ How can we thank God for you in return for all the joy we experience before our God because of you, ¹⁰ as we pray very earnestly night and day to see you face to face and to complete what is lacking in your faith?

PRAYER FOR THE CHURCH

¹¹ Now may our God and Father himself, and our Lord Jesus, direct our way to you. ¹² And may the Lord cause you to increase and overflow with love for one another and for everyone, just as we do for you. ¹³ May he make your hearts blameless in holiness before our God and Father at the coming of our Lord Jesus with all his saints. Amen.

PSALM 119:1

How happy are those whose way is blameless,
who walk according to the Lord's instruction!

2 TIMOTHY 1:1-12

GREETING

[1] Paul, an apostle of Christ Jesus by God's will, for the sake of the promise of life in Christ Jesus:

[2] To Timothy, my dearly loved son.

Grace, mercy, and peace from God the Father and Christ Jesus our Lord.

THANKSGIVING

[3] I thank God, whom I serve with a clear conscience as my ancestors did, when I constantly remember you in my prayers night and day. [4] Remembering your tears, I long to see you so that I may be filled with joy. [5] I recall your sincere faith that first lived in your grandmother Lois and in your mother Eunice and now, I am convinced, is in you also.

[6] Therefore, I remind you to rekindle the gift of God that is in you through the laying on of my hands. [7] For God has not given us a spirit of fear, but one of power, love, and sound judgment.

NOT ASHAMED OF THE GOSPEL

[8] So don't be ashamed of the testimony about our Lord, or of me his prisoner. Instead, share in suffering for the gospel, relying on the power of God. [9] He has saved us and called us with a holy calling, not according to our works, but according to his own purpose and grace, which was given to us in Christ Jesus before time began. [10] This has now been made evident through the appearing of our Savior Christ Jesus, who has abolished death and has brought life and immortality to light through the gospel. [11] For this gospel I was appointed a herald, apostle, and teacher, [12] and that is why I suffer these things. But I am not ashamed, because I know whom I have believed and am persuaded that he is able to guard what has been entrusted to me until that day.

HEBREWS 10:23-25

[23] Let us hold on to the confession of our hope without wavering, since he who promised is faithful. [24] And let us consider one another in order to provoke love and good works, [25] not neglecting to gather together, as some are in the habit of doing, but encouraging each other, and all the more as you see the day approaching.

MAY HE MAKE YOUR HEARTS BLAMELESS IN HOLINESS BEFORE OUR GOD AND FATHER.

1 THESSALONIANS 3:13

LIVING TO PLEASE GOD

1 THESSALONIANS

1 THESSALONIANS 4:1-8
THE CALL TO SANCTIFICATION

1 Additionally then, brothers and sisters, we ask and encourage you in the Lord Jesus, that as you have received instruction from us on how you should live and please God—as you are doing—do this even more. 2 For you know what commands we gave you through the Lord Jesus.

3 For this is God's will, your sanctification: that you keep away from sexual immorality, 4 that each of you knows how to control his own body in holiness and honor, 5 not with lustful passions, like the Gentiles, who don't know God. 6 This means one must not transgress against and take advantage of a brother or sister in this manner, because the Lord is an avenger of all these offenses, as we also previously told and warned you. 7 For God has not called us to impurity but to live in holiness. 8 Consequently, anyone who rejects this does not reject man, but God, who gives you his Holy Spirit.

EZEKIEL 36:26-27

26 "I will give you a new heart and put a new spirit within you; I will remove your heart of stone and give you a heart of flesh. 27 I will place my Spirit within you and cause you to follow my statutes and carefully observe my ordinances."

1 PETER 1:15-23

15 But as the one who called you is holy, you also are to be holy in all your conduct; 16 for it is written, Be holy, because I am holy. 17 If you appeal to the Father who judges impartially according to each one's work, you are to conduct yourselves in reverence during your time living as strangers. 18 For you know that you were redeemed from your empty way of life inherited from your ancestors, not with perishable things like silver or gold, 19 but with the precious blood of Christ, like that of an unblemished and spotless lamb. 20 He was foreknown before the foundation of the world but was revealed in these last times for you. 21 Through him you believe in God, who raised him from the dead and gave him glory, so that your faith and hope are in God.

22 Since you have purified yourselves by your obedience to the truth, so that you show sincere brotherly love for each other, from a pure heart love one another constantly, 23 because you have been born again—not of perishable seed but of imperishable—through the living and enduring word of God.

NOTES

150 BC   50 BC

145–50 BC

168 BC

First Jewish
community in
Thessalonica

146 BC

Thessalonica
becomes
capital of
the Roman
province of
Macedonia

42 BC

Thessalonica
declared a
free city

49–48 BC

Roman
officials flee
Rome and
settle in
Thessalonica
during Roman
Civil War

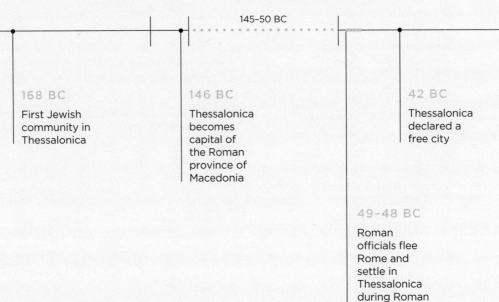

TIMELINE

THE BOOKS
OF 1 & 2
THESSALONIANS
IN HISTORY

AD 1

AD 50

AD 5

Paul born in Tarsus

AD 43

London is founded

AD 56

Paul revisits Thessalonica

5 BC

Birth of Jesus*

AD 52

Timothy returns to Thessalonica

AD 34

Paul's conversion on the road to Damascus

ca AD 50

Paul writes 1 & 2 Thessalonians

AD 50

Paul, Silas, and Timothy minister in Thessalonica and plant one of the first churches in Europe

AD 50

Emperor Claudius orders all Jews to leave Rome

AD 33

Crucifixion, resurrection, and ascension of Jesus*

Pentecost

AD 49–52

Paul's second missionary journey, with Silas

KEY

BIBLICAL DATE

EXTRABIBLICAL DATE

Though the dates in this timeline have been carefully researched, scholars disagree on the precise year of Jesus's birth and the duration of His ministry prior to His crucifixion.

AD 47–49

Paul's first missionary journey, with Barnabas and John Mark

DAY 10

THE COMFORT OF CHRIST'S COMING

1 THESSALONIANS

1 THESSALONIANS 4:9–18
LOVING AND WORKING

⁹ About brotherly love: You don't need me to write you because you yourselves are taught by God to love one another. ¹⁰ In fact, you are doing this toward all the brothers and sisters in the entire region of Macedonia. But we encourage you, brothers and sisters, to do this even more, ¹¹ to seek to lead a quiet life, to mind your own business, and to work with your own hands, as we commanded you, ¹² so that you may behave properly in the presence of outsiders and not be dependent on anyone.

THE COMFORT OF CHRIST'S COMING

¹³ We do not want you to be uninformed, brothers and sisters, concerning those who are asleep, so that you will not grieve like the rest, who have no hope. ¹⁴ For if we believe that Jesus died and rose again, in the same way, through Jesus, God will bring with him those who have fallen asleep. ¹⁵ For we say this to you by a word from the Lord: We who are still alive at the Lord's coming will certainly not precede those who have fallen asleep. ¹⁶ For the Lord himself will descend from heaven with a shout, with the archangel's voice, and with the trumpet of God, and the dead in

Christ will rise first. [17] Then we who are still alive, who are left, will be caught up together with them in the clouds to meet the Lord in the air, and so we will always be with the Lord. [18] Therefore encourage one another with these words.

JOHN 11:11-13

[11] He said this, and then he told them, "Our friend Lazarus has fallen asleep, but I'm on my way to wake him up."

[12] Then the disciples said to him, "Lord, if he has fallen asleep, he will get well."

[13] Jesus, however, was speaking about his death, but they thought he was speaking about natural sleep.

1 JOHN 4:7-17
KNOWING GOD THROUGH LOVE

[7] Dear friends, let us love one another, because love is from God, and everyone who loves has been born of God and knows God. [8] The one who does not love does not know God, because God is love. [9] God's love was revealed among us in this way: God sent his one and only Son into the world so that we might live through him. [10] Love consists in this: not that we loved God, but that he loved us and sent his Son to be the atoning sacrifice for our sins. [11] Dear friends, if God loved us in this way, we also must love one another. [12] No one has ever seen God. If we love one another, God remains in us and his love is made complete in us. [13] This is how we know that we remain in him and he in us: He has given us of his Spirit. [14] And we have seen and we testify that the Father has sent his Son as the world's Savior. [15] Whoever confesses that Jesus is the Son of God—God remains in him and he in God. [16] And we have come to know and to believe the love that God has for us.

God is love, and the one who remains in love remains in God, and God remains in him. [17] In this, love is made complete with us so that we may have confidence in the day of judgment, because as he is, so also are we in this world.

WE WILL ALWAYS BE WITH THE LORD.

1 THESSALONIANS 4:17

DAY 11

THE DAY OF THE LORD

1 THESSALONIANS

1 THESSALONIANS 5:1–11
THE DAY OF THE LORD

¹ About the times and the seasons: Brothers and sisters, you do not need anything to be written to you. ² For you yourselves know very well that the day of the Lord will come just like a thief in the night. ³ When they say, "Peace and security," then sudden destruction will come upon them, like labor pains on a pregnant woman, and they will not escape. ⁴ But you, brothers and sisters, are not in the dark, for this day to surprise you like a thief. ⁵ For you are all children of light and children of the day. We do not belong to the night or the darkness. ⁶ So then, let us not sleep, like the rest, but let us stay awake and be self-controlled. ⁷ For those who sleep, sleep at night, and those who get drunk, get drunk at night. ⁸ But since we belong to the day, let us be self-controlled and put on the armor of faith and love, and a helmet of the hope of salvation. ⁹ For God did not appoint us to wrath, but to obtain salvation through our Lord Jesus Christ, ¹⁰ who died for us, so that whether we are awake or asleep, we may live together with him. ¹¹ Therefore encourage one another and build each other up as you are already doing.

ACTS 1:6-7

[6] So when they had come together, they asked him, "Lord, are you restoring the kingdom to Israel at this time?"

[7] He said to them, "It is not for you to know times or periods that the Father has set by his own authority."

EPHESIANS 6:10-18

CHRISTIAN WARFARE

[10] Finally, be strengthened by the Lord and by his vast strength. [11] Put on the full armor of God so that you can stand against the schemes of the devil. [12] For our struggle is not against flesh and blood, but against the rulers, against the authorities, against the cosmic powers of this darkness, against evil, spiritual forces in the heavens. [13] For this reason take up the full armor of God, so that you may be able to resist in the evil day, and having prepared everything, to take your stand. [14] Stand, therefore, with truth like a belt around your waist, righteousness like armor on your chest, [15] and your feet sandaled with readiness for the gospel of peace. [16] In every situation take up the shield of faith with which you can extinguish all the flaming arrows of the evil one. [17] Take the helmet of salvation and the sword of the Spirit—which is the word of God. [18] Pray at all times in the Spirit with every prayer and request, and stay alert with all perseverance and intercession for all the saints.

NOTES

EXHORTATIONS & BLESSINGS

1 THESSALONIANS

1 THESSALONIANS 5:12-28
EXHORTATIONS AND BLESSINGS

¹² Now we ask you, brothers and sisters, to give recognition to those who labor among you and lead you in the Lord and admonish you, ¹³ and to regard them very highly in love because of their work. Be at peace among yourselves. ¹⁴ And we exhort you, brothers and sisters: warn those who are idle, comfort the discouraged, help the weak, be patient with everyone. ¹⁵ See to it that no one repays evil for evil to anyone, but always pursue what is good for one another and for all. ¹⁶ Rejoice always, ¹⁷ pray constantly, ¹⁸ give thanks in everything; for this is God's will for you in Christ Jesus. ¹⁹ Don't stifle the Spirit. ²⁰ Don't despise prophecies, ²¹ but test all things. Hold on to what is good. ²² Stay away from every kind of evil.

²³ Now may the God of peace himself sanctify you completely. And may your whole spirit, soul, and body be kept sound and blameless at the coming of our Lord Jesus Christ. ²⁴ He who calls you is faithful; he will do it. ²⁵ Brothers and sisters, pray for us also. ²⁶ Greet all the brothers and sisters with a holy kiss. ²⁷ I charge you by the Lord that this letter be read to all the brothers and sisters. ²⁸ The grace of our Lord Jesus Christ be with you.

PROVERBS 3:13-26
WISDOM BRINGS HAPPINESS

¹³ Happy is a man who finds wisdom
and who acquires understanding,
¹⁴ for she is more profitable than silver,
and her revenue is better than gold.
¹⁵ She is more precious than jewels;
nothing you desire can equal her.
¹⁶ Long life is in her right hand;
in her left, riches and honor.
¹⁷ Her ways are pleasant,
and all her paths, peaceful.
¹⁸ She is a tree of life to those who embrace her,
and those who hold on to her are happy.

¹⁹ The LORD founded the earth by wisdom
and established the heavens by understanding.
²⁰ By his knowledge the watery depths broke open,
and the clouds dripped with dew.

²¹ Maintain sound wisdom and discretion.
My son, don't lose sight of them.
²² They will be life for you
and adornment for your neck.
²³ Then you will go safely on your way;
your foot will not stumble.
²⁴ When you lie down, you will not be afraid;
you will lie down, and your sleep will be pleasant.
²⁵ Don't fear sudden danger
or the ruin of the wicked when it comes,
²⁶ for the LORD will be your confidence
and will keep your foot from a snare.

HEBREWS 13:7

Remember your leaders who have spoken God's word to you. As you carefully observe the outcome of their lives, imitate their faith.

NOTES

THANKSGIVING WILL DRAW OUR HEARTS OUT TO GOD AND KEEP US ENGAGED WITH HIM; IT WILL TAKE OUR ATTENTION FROM OURSELVES AND GIVE THE SPIRIT ROOM IN OUR HEARTS.

ANDREW MURRAY

REJOICE ALWAYS

What distractions or circumstances hindered your ability to rejoice this week? Reflect on those moments and spend time in prayer, asking God to help you turn even disappointments and sorrow into opportunities to rejoice in Him.

PRAY CONSTANTLY

Reflect on and celebrate how you incorporated prayer into your life this week. How does "constant prayer" keep you mindful of God's presence in your life?

GIVE THANKS IN EVERYTHING

What are you thankful for this week?

GRACE DAY

DAY 13   WEEK 2

Take this day to catch up on your reading, pray, and rest in the presence of the Lord.

HEBREWS 10:23-25

Let us hold on to the confession of our hope without wavering, since he who promised is faithful. And let us consider one another in order to provoke love and good works, not neglecting to gather together, as some are in the habit of doing, but encouraging each other, and all the more as you see the day approaching.

DAY 14

Scripture is God-breathed and true. When we memorize it, carry the good news of Jesus with us wherever we go.

This week, add the second part of verse 18 to the passage you're memorizing. Use the space provided to write the entire passage, then mark the symbols from the study prompts around the words to help you remember. Say the whole passage aloud before you draw, while you draw, and after you finish.

1 THESSALONIANS 5:16–18

Rejoice always, pray constantly, give thanks in everything; for this is God's will for you in Christ Jesus.

2 THESSALONIANS

*May the Lord direct your hearts to God's
love and Christ's endurance.*

2 THESSALONIANS 3:5

While there are few indicators about the date and place of the writing of 2 Thessalonians, it was probably written from Corinth around AD 50 or 51, shortly after 1 Thessalonians.

A LITTLE BACKGROUND

Following up on his first letter to the Thessalonians, Paul wrote this letter to give further clarification on how to live the Christian life in light of Christ's return. The Thessalonian believers were called to persevere and live useful lives because the return of Christ might be in the distant future.

MESSAGE & PURPOSE

Paul wrote in part to encourage the Thessalonian believers to stand firm in truth in the midst of persecution and to assure them that God would judge those afflicting them (2Th 1:6–9; 2:13–15). This short letter addresses the present needs of the congregation by focusing on four main themes:

1 THE GREATNESS OF GOD

God elects (2Th 2:13), calls (2Th 1:11; 2:14), and saves His Church, and His purpose on earth will continue until Christ's return.

2 THE SECOND COMING

The second coming is seen here in terms of the overthrowing of all evil, especially "the man of lawlessness" (2Th 2:3).

3 THE DAY OF THE LORD

The "day of the Lord" is coming, though several things must happen first, including the arrival of "the apostasy" and the revelation of "the man of lawlessness" (2Th 2:2–3).

4 LIFE AND WORK

Paul addressed the issue of people he called "busybodies" and who appeared to be idle (2Th 3:6–12). Christians are to work and not interfere with the work of others.

GIVE THANKS FOR THE BOOK OF 2 THESSALONIANS

Second Thessalonians continues and further amplifies some of the same themes found in 1 Thessalonians: persecution, sanctification, and end-time events associated with the second coming of Christ. The letter proclaims salvation in Christ—a salvation that will be consummated when Christ comes again to overthrow all evil and bring rest and glory to His own. Meanwhile, God loves His people and gives them great comfort and hope, even in the midst of persecution (2Th 2:16–17).

GOD'S JUDGMENT & GLORY

---

2 THESSALONIANS

2 THESSALONIANS 1

GREETING

[1] Paul, Silvanus, and Timothy:

To the church of the Thessalonians in God our Father and the Lord Jesus Christ.

[2] Grace to you and peace from God our Father and the Lord Jesus Christ.

GOD'S JUDGMENT AND GLORY

[3] We ought to thank God always for you, brothers and sisters, and rightly so, since your faith is flourishing and the love each one of you has for one another is increasing. [4] Therefore, we ourselves boast about you among God's churches—about your perseverance and faith in all the persecutions and afflictions that you are enduring. [5] It is clear evidence of God's righteous judgment that you will be counted worthy of God's kingdom, for which you also are suffering, [6] since it is just for God to repay with affliction those who afflict you [7] and to give relief to you who are afflicted, along with us. This will take place at the revelation of the Lord Jesus from heaven with his powerful angels, [8] when he takes vengeance with flaming fire on those who don't know God and on those who don't obey the gospel of our Lord Jesus. [9] They will pay the penalty of eternal destruction from the Lord's presence and from his glorious strength [10] on that day when he comes to be glorified by his saints and to be marveled at by all those who have believed, because our testimony among you was believed. [11] In view of this, we always pray for you that our God will make you worthy of his calling, and by his power fulfill your every desire to do good and your work produced by faith, [12] so that the name of our Lord Jesus will be glorified by you, and you by him, according to the grace of our God and the Lord Jesus Christ.

ISAIAH 66:1-4, 12-16
FINAL JUDGMENT AND JOYOUS RESTORATION

¹ This is what the LORD says:

Heaven is my throne,
and earth is my footstool.
Where could you possibly build a house for me?
And where would my resting place be?
² My hand made all these things,
and so they all came into being.

   This is the LORD's declaration.

I will look favorably on this kind of person:
one who is humble, submissive in spirit,
and trembles at my word.
³ One person slaughters an ox, another kills a person;
one person sacrifices a lamb, another breaks a dog's neck;
one person offers a grain offering, another offers
   pig's blood;
one person offers incense, another praises an idol—
all these have chosen their ways
and delight in their abhorrent practices.
⁴ So I will choose their punishment,
and I will bring on them what they dread
because I called and no one answered;
I spoke and they did not listen;
they did what was evil in my sight
and chose what I did not delight in.

  …

¹² For this is what the LORD says:

I will make peace flow to her like a river,
and the wealth of nations like a flood;
you will nurse and be carried on her hip
and bounced on her lap.
¹³ As a mother comforts her son,
so I will comfort you,
and you will be comforted in Jerusalem.
¹⁴ You will see, you will rejoice,
and you will flourish like grass;
then the LORD's power will be revealed to his servants,
but he will show his wrath against his enemies.
¹⁵ Look, the LORD will come with fire—
his chariots are like the whirlwind—
to execute his anger with fury
and his rebuke with flames of fire.
¹⁶ For the LORD will execute judgment
on all humanity with his fiery sword,
and many will be slain by the LORD.

ROMANS 8:30

And those he predestined, he also called; and those he called, he also justified; and those he justified, he also glorified.

WE ALWAYS PRAY FOR YOU THAT OUR GOD WILL MAKE YOU WORTHY OF HIS CALLING.

2 THESSALONIANS 1:11

RESISTING DECEIT

2 THESSALONIANS

2 THESSALONIANS 2:1–12
THE MAN OF LAWLESSNESS

¹ Now concerning the coming of our Lord Jesus Christ and our being gathered to him: We ask you, brothers and sisters, ² not to be easily upset or troubled, either by a prophecy or by a message or by a letter supposedly from us, alleging that the day of the Lord has come. ³ Don't let anyone deceive you in any way. For that day will not come unless the apostasy comes first and the man of lawlessness is revealed, the man doomed to destruction. ⁴ He opposes and exalts himself above every so-called god or object of worship, so that he sits in God's temple, proclaiming that he himself is God.

⁵ Don't you remember that when I was still with you I used to tell you about this? ⁶ And you know what currently restrains him, so that he will be revealed in his time. ⁷ For the mystery of lawlessness is already at work, but the one now restraining will do so until he is out of the way, ⁸ and then the lawless one will be revealed. The Lord Jesus will destroy him with the breath of his mouth and will bring him to nothing at the appearance of his coming. ⁹ The coming of the

lawless one is based on Satan's working, with every kind of miracle, both signs and wonders serving the lie, [10] and with every wicked deception among those who are perishing. They perish because they did not accept the love of the truth and so be saved. [11] For this reason God sends them a strong delusion so that they will believe the lie, [12] so that all will be condemned—those who did not believe the truth but delighted in unrighteousness.

DANIEL 11:36-37

[36] Then the king will do whatever he wants. He will exalt and magnify himself above every god, and he will say outrageous things against the God of gods. He will be successful until the time of wrath is completed, because what has been decreed will be accomplished. [37] He will not show regard for the gods of his ancestors, the god desired by women, or for any other god, because he will magnify himself above all.

EPHESIANS 5:6-14

[6] Let no one deceive you with empty arguments, for God's wrath is coming on the disobedient because of these things. [7] Therefore, do not become their partners. [8] For you were once darkness, but now you are light in the Lord. Walk as children of light— [9] for the fruit of the light consists of all goodness, righteousness, and truth— [10] testing what is pleasing to the Lord. [11] Don't participate in the fruitless works of darkness, but instead expose them. [12] For it is shameful even to mention what is done by them in secret. [13] Everything exposed by the light is made visible, [14] for what makes everything visible is light. Therefore it is said:

Get up, sleeper, and rise up from the dead,
and Christ will shine on you.

THE LIFE TO COME?

Both of Paul's letters to the Thessalonians address what happens to believers when they die. Scripture does not give us many details about the afterlife, but the information it does offer paints a deeply comforting picture.

Here are summaries of the primary biblical references concerning the life to come.

Jesus has gone to prepare a place for us, and He will come back to get us.

JN 14:2-3

We will not be limited by physical elements.

JN 20:19, 26; PHP 3:20-21

It will be like nothing we have seen, heard, or imagined.

1CO 2:9

We will see clearly face to face and know fully.

1CO 13:12

We will have new bodies. We will all be changed.

1CO 15:51-52

The dead in Christ will rise first, and we will always be with Jesus.

1TH 4:16-17

All evil and the evil one will be destroyed.

2TH 2:7-8

We will be like Christ, and we will see Him.

1JN 3:2

There will be a new heaven and a new earth.

RV 21:1

God will dwell with humanity.

RV 21:3

There will be no more death, grief, crying, or pain.

RV 21:4

STANDING FIRM

2 THESSALONIANS

2 THESSALONIANS 2:13-17
STAND FIRM

[13] But we ought to thank God always for you, brothers and sisters loved by the Lord, because from the beginning God has chosen you for salvation through sanctification by the Spirit and through belief in the truth. [14] He called you to this through our gospel, so that you might obtain the glory of our Lord Jesus Christ. [15] So then, brothers and sisters, stand firm and hold to the traditions you were taught, whether by what we said or what we wrote.

[16] May our Lord Jesus Christ himself and God our Father, who has loved us and given us eternal encouragement and good hope by grace, [17] encourage your hearts and strengthen you in every good work and word.

2 THESSALONIANS 3:1-5
PRAY FOR US

[1] In addition, brothers and sisters, pray for us that the word of the Lord may spread rapidly and be honored, just as it was with you, [2] and that we may be delivered from wicked and evil people, for not all have faith. [3] But the Lord is faithful; he will strengthen you and guard you from the evil one. [4] We have confidence in the Lord about you, that you are doing and will continue to do what we command. [5] May the Lord direct your hearts to God's love and Christ's endurance.

PROVERBS 10:25

When the whirlwind passes,
the wicked are no more,
but the righteous are secure forever.

1 PETER 5:6-11

[6] Humble yourselves, therefore, under the mighty hand of God, so that he may exalt you at the proper time, [7] casting all your cares on him, because he cares about you. [8] Be sober-minded, be alert. Your adversary the devil is prowling around like a roaring lion, looking for anyone he can devour. [9] Resist him, firm in the faith, knowing that the same kind of sufferings are being experienced by your fellow believers throughout the world.

[10] The God of all grace, who called you to his eternal glory in Christ, will himself restore, establish, strengthen, and support you after you have suffered a little while. [11] To him be dominion forever. Amen.

NOTES

A CALL TO RESPONSIBILITY

2 THESSALONIANS

2 THESSALONIANS 3:6–15
WARNING AGAINST IRRESPONSIBLE BEHAVIOR

[6] Now we command you, brothers and sisters, in the name of our Lord Jesus Christ, to keep away from every brother or sister who is idle and does not live according to the tradition received from us. [7] For you yourselves know how you should imitate us: We were not idle among you; [8] we did not eat anyone's food free of charge; instead, we labored and toiled, working night and day, so that we would not be a burden to any of you. [9] It is not that we don't have the right to support, but we did it to make ourselves an example to you so that you would imitate us. [10] In fact, when we were with you, this is what we commanded you: "If anyone isn't willing to work, he should not eat." [11] For we hear that there are some among you who are idle. They are not busy but busybodies. [12] Now we command and exhort such people by the Lord Jesus Christ to work quietly and provide for themselves. [13] But as for you, brothers and sisters, do not grow weary in doing good.

[14] If anyone does not obey our instruction in this letter, take note of that person; don't associate with him, so that he may be ashamed. [15] Yet don't consider him as an enemy, but warn him as a brother.

DO NOT GROW WEARY
IN DOING GOOD.

2 THESSALONIANS 3:13

2 CORINTHIANS 11:5-9

⁵ Now I consider myself in no way inferior to those "super-apostles." ⁶ Even if I am untrained in public speaking, I am certainly not untrained in knowledge. Indeed, we have in every way made that clear to you in everything. ⁷ Or did I commit a sin by humbling myself so that you might be exalted, because I preached the gospel of God to you free of charge? ⁸ I robbed other churches by taking pay from them to minister to you. ⁹ When I was present with you and in need, I did not burden anyone, since the brothers who came from Macedonia supplied my needs. I have kept myself, and will keep myself, from burdening you in any way.

HEBREWS 13:20-21
BENEDICTION AND FAREWELL

²⁰ Now may the God of peace, who brought up from the dead our Lord Jesus—the great Shepherd of the sheep—through the blood of the everlasting covenant, ²¹ equip you with everything good to do his will, working in us what is pleasing in his sight, through Jesus Christ, to whom be glory forever and ever. Amen.

FINAL GREETINGS

2 THESSALONIANS

2 THESSALONIANS 3:16–18
FINAL GREETINGS

[16] May the Lord of peace himself give you peace always in every way. The Lord be with all of you. [17] I, Paul, am writing this greeting with my own hand, which is an authenticating mark in every letter; this is how I write. [18] The grace of our Lord Jesus Christ be with you all.

PHILIPPIANS 4:6–7

[6] Don't worry about anything, but in everything, through prayer and petition with thanksgiving, present your requests to God. [7] And the peace of God, which surpasses all understanding, will guard your hearts and minds in Christ Jesus.

COLOSSIANS 3:12–17
THE CHRISTIAN LIFE

[12] Therefore, as God's chosen ones, holy and dearly loved, put on compassion, kindness, humility, gentleness, and patience, [13] bearing with one another and forgiving one another if anyone has a grievance against another. Just as the Lord has forgiven you, so you are also to forgive. [14] Above all, put on love, which is the perfect bond of unity. [15] And let the peace of Christ, to which you were also called in one body, rule your hearts. And be thankful. [16] Let the word of Christ dwell richly among you, in all wisdom teaching and admonishing one another through psalms, hymns, and spiritual songs, singing to God with gratitude in your hearts. [17] And whatever you do, in word or in deed, do everything in the name of the Lord Jesus, giving thanks to God the Father through him.

NOTES

THERE IS NOT ONE BLADE OF GRASS, THERE IS NO COLOR IN THIS WORLD THAT IS NOT INTENDED TO MAKE US REJOICE.

JOHN CALVIN

REJOICE ALWAYS

How did you find joy in Jesus and in God's Word this week?

PRAY CONSTANTLY

What distractions or circumstances kept you from seeking the Lord in prayer?

GIVE THANKS IN EVERYTHING

After reading about your security in Christ this week, what did you you learn that compels you to give thanks?

DATE

GRACE
DAY

DAY 20   WEEK 3

Take this day to catch up on your reading, pray, and rest in the presence of the Lord.

---

1 PETER 5:10

The God of all grace, who called you to his eternal glory in Christ, will himself restore, establish, strengthen, and support you after you have suffered a little while.

WEEKLY TRUTH

DAY 21

Scripture is God-breathed and true. When we memorize it, carry the good news of Jesus with us wherever we go.

In this final week, write down the full memorization passage by hand three times. Then try going on a short walk—even if it's just around the house—and repeating the full passage aloud.

1 THESSALONIANS 5:16–18

Rejoice always, pray constantly, give thanks in everything; for this is God's will for you in Christ Jesus.

1

2

3

Now may the God of peace himself sanctify you completely. And may your whole spirit, soul, and body be kept sound and blameless at the coming of our Lord Jesus Christ.

HE WHO CALLS YOU IS

FAITHFUL; HE WILL DO IT.

1 THESSALONIANS 5:23–24

CSB BOOK ABBREVIATIONS

OLD TESTAMENT

GN Genesis

EX Exodus

LV Leviticus

NM Numbers

DT Deuteronomy

JOS Joshua

JDG Judges

RU Ruth

1SM 1 Samuel

2SM 2 Samuel

1KG 1 Kings

2KG 2 Kings

1CH 1 Chronicles

2CH 2 Chronicles

EZR Ezra

NEH Nehemiah

EST Esther

JB Job

PS Psalms

PR Proverbs

EC Ecclesiastes

SG Song of Solomon

IS Isaiah

JR Jeremiah

LM Lamentations

EZK Ezekiel

DN Daniel

HS Hosea

JL Joel

AM Amos

OB Obadiah

JNH Jonah

MC Micah

NAH Nahum

HAB Habakkuk

ZPH Zephaniah

HG Haggai

ZCH Zechariah

MAL Malachi

NEW TESTAMENT

MT Matthew

MK Mark

LK Luke

JN John

AC Acts

RM Romans

1CO 1 Corinthians

2CO 2 Corinthians

GL Galatians

EPH Ephesians

PHP Philippians

COL Colossians

1TH 1 Thessalonians

2TH 2 Thessalonians

1TM 1 Timothy

2TM 2 Timothy

TI Titus

PHM Philemon

HEB Hebrews

JMS James

1PT 1 Peter

2PT 2 Peter

1JN 1 John

2JN 2 John

3JN 3 John

JD Jude

RV Revelation

BIBLIOGRAPHY

Biblia. "Epistle to Philemon." Accessed October 2020, https://biblia.com/factbook/Epistle-to-Philemon.

Blum, Edwin A., and Trevin Wax, eds. "The Second Missionary Journey of Paul." In *CSB Study Bible: Notes.* Nashville: Holman Bible Publishers, 2017.

Bouwsma, William J. *John Calvin: A Sixteenth-Century Portrait.* New York: Oxford University Press, 1988.

Chambers, Oswald. *My Utmost for His Highest.* Uhrichsville: Barbour Publishing, Inc., 1963.

Keener, Craig S. *Romans: A New Covenant Commentary.* Cambridge: Lutterworth Press, 2011.

Murray, Andrew. *The Prayer Life: Persevering in Prayer.* Abbotsford: Life Sentence Publishing, Inc., 2018.

Zondervan Academic. "What You Might Not Know About Paul's Letters." Last modified March 1, 2016, https://zondervanacademic.com/blog/what-you-might-not-know-about-pauls-letters.

SHE
READS
TRUTH
PODCAST

God's Word is for you and for now.

Join our founders Raechel and Amanda in conversation that delights in the beauty, goodness, and truth found in Scripture. Created to complement the current community reading plan, the She Reads Truth podcast will encourage you on your commute to work, while you're out for a walk, or at home making dinner. Subscribe today and don't miss an episode!

JOIN US ON APPLE PODCASTS OR YOUR PREFERRED STREAMING PLATFORM

WE'VE BEEN THERE.

Knowing where to start reading the Bible can be hard. In a world of so many distractions, constant notifications, and endless to-do lists, it's easy to slip into a rut when it comes to reading God's Word. But you don't have to stay there.

Be a woman in the Word every day with the She Reads Truth Subscription Box. For just $20 a month, you'll get each brand new Study Book we create delivered right to your door, plus exclusive perks like free gifts, early access to sales, and more! Our monthly delivery service sets you up to engage with God's Word on the good days, the bad days, and all the days in between. We'll do the planning for you, so all you have to do is show up, open God's Word, and then do it again tomorrow.

USE CODE BOX20 FOR 20% OFF

YOUR FIRST MONTH'S BOX!

SUBSCRIPTION.SHOPSHEREADSTRUTH.COM

WHERE DID I STUDY?

O HOME
O OFFICE
O COFFEE SHOP
O CHURCH
O A FRIEND'S HOUSE
O OTHER:

WHAT WAS I LISTENING TO?

ARTIST:

SONG:

PLAYLIST:

WHEN DID I STUDY?

O MORNING
O AFTERNOON
O NIGHT

HOW DID I FIND DELIGHT IN GOD'S WORD?

WHAT WAS HAPPENING IN MY LIFE?

WHAT WAS HAPPENING IN THE WORLD?

MONTH	DAY	YEAR

END DATE